For more information please contact: info@jwedholmdesign.ca.

First paperback edition October 2018.

Book design & illustrations by Jaime Wedholm.
Featuring phrases by SippingTHIS, LLC (pages 25, 49 & 69).

ISBN 978-1-7200-7846-3 (paperback)

www.jwedholmdesign.ca

Acknowledgements

Nothing I say or write will ever properly express the gratitude I have for the support of my family, friends and community in creating this, my first book. I am hopeful that this will suffice!

To my husband who while supporting my book journey probably cursed me at length for obsessing over intricate design details and spending far more time on my passion project than either of us would have guessed. I couldn't have accomplished this goal without your love and patience... And it shouldn't go without mentioning all the nights I tucked away at the coffee shop juggling client projects while creating this book - you are a rock star for giving me the space and time to 'do my thang'!

To my friends and family... Thanks for kicking my ass when I am in doubt. Thanks for infusing logic when I am irrational. Thanks for accepting me with all my crazy-ass quirks! Thank you for encouraging me to take this book from "Maybe one day", to "Now damn it!".
To Christina... Thank you for being a true friend, for happily receiving my endless texts, for always being so damn level-headed and for your honesty that is always coated in compassion.
To Dana... Thank you for sharing your publishing knowledge with me, your help sure made things a helluva lot easier than if I had done it alone!

To my sister...Your enthusiasm for this project and hilarious "Oh my f*ing god I love this one!!" texts, fueled my excitement as we approached launch! I love you.

Alright, I think that sums up my gushings of gratitude
– Yes, I know *gushings* isn't a word ;)

Now turn the page, pour a glass of vino and get your colour on!

Sketch your wine-themed colouring page idea here!

Enter for a chance to be featured in *Sip. Colour. Smile.* Volume 2.

Snap a photo and submit to info@jwedholmdesign.ca
Submissions deadline: January 31, 2019.

11

Sketch your wine-themed colouring page idea here!

Enter for a chance to be featured in *Sip. Colour. Smile.* Volume 2.

Snap a photo and submit to info@jwedholmdesign.ca
Submissions deadline: January 31, 2019.

Sketch your wine-themed colouring page idea here!

Enter for a chance to be featured in *Sip. Colour. Smile.* Volume 2.

Snap a photo and submit to info@jwedholmdesign.ca
Submissions deadline: January 31, 2019.

Spread your wings & wine

Sketch your wine-themed colouring page idea here!

Enter for a chance to be featured in *Sip. Colour. Smile.* Volume 2.

Snap a photo and submit to info@jwedholmdesign.ca
Submissions deadline: January 31, 2019.

WINE
doesn't make me
DRUNK
it makes me
AWESOME

Sketch your wine-themed colouring page idea here!

Enter for a chance to be featured in *Sip. Colour. Smile.* Volume 2.

Snap a photo and submit to info@jwedholmdesign.ca
Submissions deadline: January 31, 2019.

When the stars align, let there be WINE

Sketch your wine-themed colouring page idea here!

Enter for a chance to be featured in *Sip. Colour. Smile.* Volume 2.

Snap a photo and submit to info@jwedholmdesign.ca
Submissions deadline: January 31, 2019.

IT'S WINE:30

Sketch your wine-themed colouring page idea here!

Enter for a chance to be featured in *Sip. Colour. Smile.* Volume 2.

Snap a photo and submit to info@jwedholmdesign.ca
Submissions deadline: January 31, 2019.

Sketch your wine-themed colouring page idea here!

Enter for a chance to be featured in *Sip. Colour. Smile.* Volume 2.

Snap a photo and submit to info@jwedholmdesign.ca
Submissions deadline: January 31, 2019.

39

Sketch your wine-themed colouring page idea here!

Enter for a chance to be featured in *Sip. Colour. Smile.* Volume 2.

Snap a photo and submit to info@jwedholmdesign.ca
Submissions deadline: January 31, 2019.

But First... Wine!

Sketch your wine-themed colouring page idea here!

Enter for a chance to be featured in *Sip. Colour. Smile.* Volume 2.

Snap a photo and submit to info@jwedholmdesign.ca
Submissions deadline: January 31, 2019.

Sketch your wine-themed colouring page idea here!

Enter for a chance to be featured in *Sip. Colour. Smile.* Volume 2.

Snap a photo and submit to info@jwedholmdesign.ca
Submissions deadline: January 31, 2019.

GET YOUR ZIN ON

Sketch your wine-themed colouring page idea here!

Enter for a chance to be featured in *Sip. Colour. Smile.* Volume 2.

Snap a photo and submit to info@jwedholmdesign.ca
Submissions deadline: January 31, 2019.

55

Sketch your wine-themed colouring page idea here!

Enter for a chance to be featured in *Sip. Colour. Smile.* Volume 2.

Snap a photo and submit to info@jwedholmdesign.ca
Submissions deadline: January 31, 2019.

59

Sketch your wine-themed colouring page idea here!

Enter for a chance to be featured in *Sip. Colour. Smile.* Volume 2.

Snap a photo and submit to info@jwedholmdesign.ca
Submissions deadline: January 31, 2019.

63

Cheers!

Sketch your wine-themed colouring page idea here!

Enter for a chance to be featured in *Sip. Colour. Smile.* Volume 2.

Snap a photo and submit to info@jwedholmdesign.ca
Submissions deadline: January 31, 2019.

Don't need a GLASS of wine. The BOTTLE & a STRAW will do.

Made in the USA
Monee, IL
07 July 2022

99215328R00039